May 2007

Mark—

Thank you for being a
leader in service to life.

Jane

Leadership in Service to Life

We Are Divine Our Essence Is Love

Timeless Truths for Today's Leaders

Jane C. Nebelung

WingSpan Press

Printed in the United States of America

Cover art: Trinity Knot design used with permission of
            Solvar Irish Jewellry Ltd.

Cover design: www.JStewartDesigns.com

Published by WingSpan Press, Livermore, CA
www.wingspanpress.com

The WingSpan name, logo and colophon are the
trademarks of WingSpan Publishing.

ISBN 978-1-59594-133-6

First edition 2007

Library of Congress Control Number 2007922217

This book is humbly dedicated to:

Andrew, whose questions about life, death and God in August 2006 gave me the courage to step into my life's purpose.

Wagner who showed us the meaning of unconditional love and the joy of life.

All people who choose to liberate their souls and live their lives in love, creating a path that enables others to do the same. You are the true leaders of humanity who will create a world of peace and prosperity, heaven on earth for all.

Leaders who understand their power, have the courage to acknowledge and nurture our divine nature, and willingly accept the challenge to be catalysts for world change.

Acknowledgements

It is no mistake that I begin writing this book on November 2, 2006. In the Catholic tradition, today is All Souls Day. I am grateful that both Kuan Yin, who hears the cries of the world, and Kali Ma, the mother who liberates souls, are with me as guides in this process.

I am grateful to my parents, Jane and Archie Corrigan, for every experience they gave me. These experiences provided the context for who I choose to be today.

Numerous books and sources contributed to my understanding of both spiritual and business concepts. I am grateful for living in a time in which this breadth of wisdom is available. If I fail to explicitly acknowledge a source in the text, it is because I no longer remember where I learned the concept or because I have read the concept in multiple authors, not because of an intentional omission of the original source. Among the many authors that have shaped my reflections and the concepts in this book:

Arbinger Institute	Judi Neal
Warren Bennis	Harrison Owen
Peter Block	Parker Palmer
Gregg Braden	Robert Quinn
Elizabeth Denton	John Randolf Price
Paul Ferrini	Michael Ray
Matthew Fox	Colin Tipping
Daniel Goleman	Eckhart Tolle
Ronald Heifetz	James Twyman

David Hawkins	Neale Donald Walsh
Ronald Jue	Margaret Wheatley
Robert Kegan	Marianne Williamson
Carolyn Myss	Gary Zukav

I am blessed that several of these authors are also wonderful colleagues and friends: Liz Denton, Ron Jue and Judi Neal.

Time and love given in thoughtful review made this book clearer and richer. I appreciate the comments and suggestions that Jennifer Berlin, Liz Denton, Deborah Moshier-Dunn, Doreen Goodnough, Elizabeth Hall, Trish Pratt, John Wyche, and David Zacchei provided. Elizabeth also contributed substantially to Chapter 6, "Order from Chaos," both through our many conversations over the years and in the section, "The Future." As a wonderful friend, Liz Denton reviewed the book not once, but three times, the first time sitting at my dining room table and reading it out loud with me. I greatly appreciate her continued support and wisdom.

Most of all, I am deeply grateful for my husband, Alexander, and the many friends and colleagues who are part of my path. Their presence enables me to see who I really am and to reflect on my experience. They share my excitement for this book. They include Anna Aramini, Debra Castelluccio, Allison Davis, Elizabeth Hall, Patty Hall, Carol Orticari, Martha Summerville, Kusala Tibbitts, Mara Senese, Lisa Steinberg, and R. Michael Smith.

I am grateful that at the last moment, my editor, Mary Redmond, challenged me to include my story in the first chapter. Sharing my experience provided the much-needed context for the content of the book.

January 12, 2007

We have been telling the people that this is the eleventh hour. Now you must go back and tell the people that this is the hour.

There are things to be considered: Where are you living? What are you doing? What are your relationships? Are you in the right relation? Where is your water? Know your garden.

It is time to speak your truth. Create your community. Be good to each other. And do not look outside yourself for the leader. The leader is within. This could be a good time!

There is a river flowing very fast. It is so great and swift that there are those who will be afraid. They will try to hold onto the shore. They will feel they are being torn apart and they will suffer greatly. Know the river has its destination.

The elders say we must let go of the shore and push off and into the river, keep our eyes open and our head above the water. See who is in there with you and celebrate.

At this time in history, we are to take nothing personally, least of all ourselves. For the moment that we do, our spiritual growth and journey come to a halt.

The time of the lone wolf is over. Gather yourselves!

Banish the word "struggle" from your attitude and your vocabulary. All that you do now must be done in a sacred manner and in celebration.

"We are the ones we've been waiting for..."

The Elders, Hopi Nation, Oraibi, Arizona
November 2005

Contents

FOREWORD

Jane Nebelung has written a remarkable book -- one of great clarity and precision. Weaving together the riches of ancient wisdom, quantum physics, universal spiritual principles, and leadership and organizational practices, she gives us a guide, a spiritual roadmap by which we can become more conscious and aware of our decisions and our choices and their consequences.

This is a book for each of us, whether or not we have the "official" role as a leader in an organization. We all are involved in many aspects of leading and serving others in our day-to-day lives, but for the leaders of our organizations, *Leadership in Service to Life* is especially relevant in showing the way to bring more consciousness and humanity into our work lives. Through her thinking and writing, Nebelung herself is a leader in service to life and a potential catalyst for world change.

Elizabeth Denton, Ph.D., co-author of *A Spiritual Audit of Corporate America*

1

I TRUST MY OWN POWER TO CREATE

The reasonable person adapts her/ himself to the world. The unreasonable person persists in trying to adapt the world to her/ himself. All progress depends on the unreasonable person.

Adapted from George Bernard Shaw

This first chapter is really my preface. The chapter title captures my belief that through this book, I can be a catalyst for world change. You can, too. This book ends 10 years of using language that hid what I know to be true. With this book, I am opening to new possibilities for myself, and I hope that you open to new possibilities as well.

My full-time work in business began in 1978 in a small stock brokerage in Hartford, Connecticut. At this time, if I remember correctly, the Dow was at about 1,200 and

40 million shares was a busy day. Trades were reconciled manually based on hand-written sheets from the floor of the stock exchanges that were sent nightly to Hartford via Greyhound bus. I supervised the department that did this reconciliation, lowering the error rate from around 5 percent of the transactions to less than 1 percent. I was making $175.00 per week at the time. Eighteen months later, I was fired when I asked for a $50.00 per week raise instead of the $25.00 that they offered – my New York counterparts were making around $275.00 per week. Welcome to the world of business.

My background is in Industrial Organizational Psychology, the application of psychological concepts to business and organizations. My spiritual path began in the early 1990s. I was working at Aetna at the time. My initial positions with Aetna centered in Strategic Human Resource Management. I later moved into positions in Organizational Development, Learning and Change. In these positions, I had the opportunity to work with the corporation's senior executives and the chairman.

In 1992, Meg Wheatley published her book, *Leadership and the New Science*. It changed how I view organizations and change: I no longer believed in "top-down" leadership, the need for hierarchical control and the concept of "change management." While not always successful at influencing the executives that I worked with to apply these concepts, I was blessed to have many opportunities to apply and expand them over the years in my own leadership roles. I saw their power first hand.

A year later, James Redfield published *The Celestine Prophecy.* My first reaction was, "this is everything that the Catholic Church doesn't want us to know." My second thought was that *The Celestine Prophecy* and *Leadership and the New Science* were saying the same thing: Life has a spiritual basis, and when we honor our spiritual nature, our potential is limitless.

In 1994, I attended one of Meg Wheatley's dialogues, "Self-Organizing Systems: The New Science of Participation." The dialogue was held in Snowmass, Utah. As I was looking up the mountain, out of the window of my hotel room at the beauty of the rock-faced cliff and the snow at dusk, I heard a voice very clearly say, "You are to be a leader in this movement." And so it began.

In May 1995, I chaired a symposium at the annual conference of the Society of Industrial Organizational Psychology entitled, "New Science: An Exploration, Implications and Opportunities for I/O Psychology." In my presentation, I shared how we applied these concepts in the change model we developed at Aetna. They are still key foundations for my work with organizational change.

It was around this time that I met Judi Neal and became involved with the Association for Spirit at Work, making several presentations over the years at chapter meetings. But, I was not able to bring my insights and ideas into Aetna except behind closed doors with trusted colleagues.

One of the executives that I had several conversations with was Michael Stephen, who, at that time, was Chairman of

Aetna International. I met Michael in 1990 while he was president of Aetna Canada, and I facilitated a meeting in Toronto for Aetna's Asia-Pacific Region executive team. Michael had turned Aetna Canada around, enabling it to become profitable by leading the organization using spiritual principles. His story is in his book, *Spirituality in Business: The Hidden Success Factor.* Michael and I talked about what he did with Aetna Canada and, at the same time, he cautioned me not to use the "S" word with my business colleagues.

Michael's greatest gift of wisdom to me: Anything that I suggest to executives as a course of action needs to be clearly tied to the business strategy and with business results. This has served me very well in my career.

This wisdom initiated my research of the published literature on the behaviors and practices that drive business profitability, essentially seeking what are *the* causes of business financial success. As a psychologist with an interest in physiology stemming from my undergraduate years, I came to the conclusion that there are five key human factors in business success: purpose and meaning, connection and participation, growth and development, respect, and self-determination and choice. And oh, by the way, these psychological needs are hardwired into our brain. It was my personal spiritual path that made the connection between these business success factors and universal spiritual principles.

I remember a staff meeting with my executive peers at Aetna around 1999. A colleague suggested that we put "the fear of God" into the employees. I emphatically replied, "This is the *last* thing that we want to do. We will shut down their creative thinking, which is what we need right now." I had never replied with such passion before and I think we were all surprised by what I said; I know I was. My façade was beginning to crack.

Judi Neal and I became close friends, but I continued to hide that my work in business was based in spiritual principles. This always felt deceptive.

For the last 15 years, I have read about, and from, many spiritual traditions. You might say I was sampling from a grand buffet of offerings. I frequently criticized myself for my lack of discipline in any one practice. I know now that I was meant to "dabble." In my reading, it became clearer and clearer that while spiritual practices are different, at their essence, they are saying three things: We are one. We are a unique manifestation of the divine. We have a free will.

Fast forward. Prudential acquired CIGNA's retirement business in 2003 and just prior to that, the department I was leading was eliminated to reduce expenses. I looked at a number of positions and began consulting. In May 2006, I was about to receive an offer for a "very big job" with a major financial services company. The week I was waiting for the offer, the knot in my stomach was growing bigger and bigger and tighter and tighter. I finally came to realize that I couldn't go back into corporate America the way it was currently operating. I knew too much and couldn't pretend otherwise by using traditional, mainstream methods in my work. I needed to be explicit when working with leaders that using universal spiritual principles to lead our businesses *is what creates* financial abundance.

In August, I was sitting on the stairs at the shallow end of a pool with 14-year-old Andrew. Andrew's family lived across the street from us when his father committed suicide. Andrew was four or five at the time. He learned the truth of his father's death in 2006 and he was grappling with questions such as: "What is death?" "Where is my father?" "Will I see him again?" "Who is God?" I answered his questions to the best of my ability.

A couple of weeks later, I began reading Michael Ray's book, *The Highest Goal: The Secret that Sustains You in Every Moment*. It is based on his Stanford University Creativity Course. On page 8 of the introduction, he asks the reader to recall the most meaningful thing that s/he did in the last week or so. He then instructs the reader to continue to ask the question, "Why is this so important, so meaningful to me?" for each successive answer until s/he gets to one word. I ask these questions based on my conversation with Andrew. My one word was "christos," meaning "christ," the anointed one. As divine beings, we are all "anointed ones."

Only now do I fully understand my purpose and what I am to bring to the world, especially to business. I am to bring the truth: That we are divine, that our essence is love. I am to show each of you the light of love that is within you. I am to bring the truth that supporting and serving life is the source of all expansion and success, including financial abundance. Service to life recognizes our divinity and uses the universal truths of oneness, uniqueness and free will to guide actions. Business leadership based in these truths creates financial abundance. The only question we ever need to ask ourselves is: "Does this serve life?"

Business can be a catalyst to change the world. The chaos that we are witnessing in the world demands that we take a radical approach to leading and managing our businesses. In this sense, radical means "root cause," an approach to business that addresses the very nature of our humanity, our divinity. We can live our divinity in business.

This is a book about liberation, our liberation. It is a mirror to show you who you are, the essence of love that is the core of your being. It is my intention that the book be a catalyst for humanity to reclaim our divinity and create a world of peace and prosperity, heaven on earth. I hope you are inspired to choose to bring humanity's divinity out of the shadow and into the light. Each of us is a potential instrument of world change from exactly where we are.

This is a book about response-ability, our ability to respond, and taking responsibility as the divine creators that we are. Every moment we are creators. We choose either love or fear. We can choose to step into our power that comes from within and to co-create our life through love rather than fear.

Some of you may be new to a spiritual path. Others may be deeply engaged in spiritual practice. Either way, I have no desire to convince you of anything. I do hope to offer you a simple way to see a world of new possibilities and invite you to join in transforming humanity. In this way, we are all leaders, and can radically change the world and our experience of life. It does not matter whether you have a "position" of leadership. We all impact the world by our thoughts and actions, how we choose to "show up." Whether you talk about conscious, enlightened, resonant, authentic or servant leadership, they are all essentially the same. We lead from wherever we are. Leadership is a state of being that results when one masters oneself. By our presence as leaders we enable others to act and live life as a full expression of divinity. As leaders, we always have the power to change a situation.

This book is intentionally brief. Consider it a summary of key points. I touch on many concepts, so it is like taking a microscopically thin slice across the top of each book in a library of spiritual and business practices. It begins with a brief summary of universal spiritual teachings and principles. I hope I have captured the essence of their truths. I will not be giving you spiritual practices or things to do; rather, I will be sharing principles and how they might be applied in business. At the end of the book is a resource section.

As a book of my reflections, these are my insights and experiences and a few "ah-ha" moments. While reading, I invite you to do your own reflection, to go within and take only what resonates with your own truth. It is my prayer that as you touch your truths, you move deeper into wholeness and integration of your body, mind, emotions and spirit. Wholeness is your integrity of being and living in full consciousness.

This is a book of hope, a reminder of who we are, of our potential. It is about the possible future that we can create. Our role, if we accept it, is to generate and expand the love that is and that we are. To provide inspiration and to support mastery of living your own divinity, I hope that you reach for this book again and again.

Welcome to the journey home.

Namaste
The Divine in me honors the Divine in you

2

THE KEYS TO THE KINGDOM

God is love and he who abides in love abides in God and God in him.

1 John 4:16

The spiritual literature encompasses thousands of years and millions of pages. I do not profess to be an expert in any one tradition. The summary in this chapter is at a very high level to create common language and concepts that I will use later in my discussions about business. The major conclusions from my reading and reflections on my experience were captured in the first chapter. I believe there is a common, implicit thread in the spiritual literature, what I am calling universal truths or principles: oneness, uniqueness and free will. These are the keys to the kingdom, heaven on earth.

Who is, or what is God? God goes by many names: Allah, Yahweh, Abba, Spirit, All That Is, I Am That I Am, Source. I'm referring to all of these labels that attempt to define the indefinable.

God is not a "who." God is a "what." God is the energy of love that generates, nurtures and sustains all of creation and life. In our attempt to understand the mystery of what God is, we made God a "who" with human qualities.

God is the energy of love ever present, the sacred in all of creation. Because God is everywhere, the energy of love is everywhere, in every atom and cell of every object and every being in the universe. Because God/Love is every object and every being, we are one as part of God/Love. The belief that we are apart from, that we are separate from God/Love and every object and every being is an illusion that we have created. It is we who have chosen to veil our oneness and God's/Love's full expression.

God is Love is Life. Since everything in the universe is of God, it may be said that God is Life. How can we honor God? By honoring and nurturing any and all of creation, by serving Life with Love. There is no greater power than love.

We all have personal meaning and experiences associated with the word "God." So, for the remainder of the book, I will use Source or Spirit to mean God/Love.

NATURE OF HUMANITY

Who are we? We are divine beings having a human experience! It is through our physical bodies that Spirit has a human experience. We are so much more than our physical selves. Our individual soul, our connection to Source, is for each of us a unique manifestation of the divine, of Source. The purpose of our existence is to experience the joy of choosing to re-member, to rejoin and become one with Spirit, to be healed. Healing is bringing together and integrating the totality of our beingness as humans – our body, mind, emotions and spirit. As we are healed, we bring Spirit's presence into the world. It is time to remember and believe that we are divine.

Each of us has a unique form of love to bring to the world. Our unique love is a gift of Spirit; we are a conduit for Spirit's love. Our power is the love within us focused or directed (or stifled) by our free will. Anyone who chooses their love which, is their power, is a leader serving life. Another way of thinking about this is that we come into this world uniquely hardwired and with the software to fulfill our purpose. As Spirit, we bring our unique form and gift of love. When business practices attempt to create conformity to some standard, we diminish this uniqueness.

As divine beings, with Source we co-create life. In our attempt to understand what we experience, we make things complicated. They aren't. Life is governed by three simple, universal principles or truths:

- We are One, intimately connected with all of creation.
- We are each a unique manifestation or expression of Spirit, a unique expression of Love.
- We have a free will to create our life, to choose our experiences.

We have learned through quantum physics and complexity theory that simple rules generate complex systems. The complexity we witness and experience in life results from these three simple truths that are the laws of life in dynamic relationship with one another and connected by the energy of love.

This is why I chose the Trinity Knot pictured on the cover and throughout the book as the symbol for Leadership in Service to Life. The three loops intertwined with the heart represent oneness, uniqueness and free will connected by the energy of love. When all three are simultaneously considered, the resulting actions will be in the best interest of humanity.

Or, if you prefer, we can use a triangle to depict this dynamic relationship.

Oneness

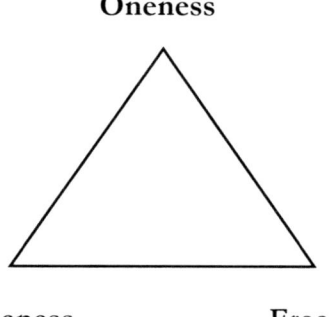

Uniqueness   **Free Will**

Every other spiritual concept and practice is a derivative of these three principles, these laws of life, laws of love. These include the Ten Commandments in the Judeo-Christian tradition, The Pillars of Islam, The Eightfold Path of Buddhism, the Ancient Wisdom Teachings in the Native/Shamanic traditions, and others.

Contrary to popular understanding, statements such as "an eye for an eye," are not about advocating revenge. Originally, in Judaism, these concepts were meant to teach limits on retribution. The deeper lesson is that what you do to others, you do to yourself. When we do something harmful or nurturing to ourselves, we are harming or nurturing all of creation. This is why the Buddhists teach, "Do no harm." This is the Law of Dharma, the highest Law of Life. We are one. When we ignore our interconnectedness, we ignore our divinity and we diminish who we are and deny our power to create.

Reflect for a moment and seek the presence of these principles in your life:

- ◆ Am I honoring my oneness, my connection and interdependence with life, with others?
- ◆ Am I honoring my own and others' uniqueness, our unique expression of love?
- ◆ Am I respecting my own and others' free will, our right to choose?

As you read through the rest of this chapter, I invite you to think about your leadership and business practices. Do they simultaneously respect our oneness, uniqueness and free will?

SURRENDER

Surrender is accepting our divine nature, that we are divine beings, that we are one with Source and with all of creation. We *are* love. The love of Source is within each of us; it is the energy of our life. Enlightenment is choosing to live this truth in each and every moment. As love, we *are* a part of God. Surrender does not mean "give up." Surrender means allowing divine will and love to work through us, without interference from our belief that we are "only human." We do not need to go through religious intermediaries to reach Source because collectively we *are* Spirit. In surrender, we become an instrument of Spirit, a channel for divine love. Once we accept our own divinity, we have the power to acknowledge and accept the divinity of others.

When, in the face of hardship, we ask, "How could God let this happen?" we are denying our responsibility in creation, projecting the event onto "God." Instead, we can ask ourselves, "Why did we choose this in our life?" Through our free will and our interdependent thoughts with others, we created the experience. Creation is *always* ours. We do it either consciously or unconsciously. No one or no thing, especially God/Love, is doing anything *to* us. We are doing it to ourselves: Sometimes we can be our own worst enemies!

NATURE OF CREATION AND REALITY

As humans, in the disbelief of our *divine* nature, we have chosen to experience life as a duality of two realities: Source and ego. Ego is the self-image of our physical being, our perception of our self as separate. This illusion hides our light, our divinity, creating shadow. The biblical story of the Garden of Eden and original sin (sin means "missing the mark" or "moving away from God") are metaphors for our choice to sever our connection to Spirit. We "miss" the connection or mark. Duality, polarity and separation are illusions.

In our lives, we can choose to experience ego or divinity, which includes our oneness, uniqueness and free will. In other words, do we choose to identify with our divinity or do we choose to identify with our body and our ego (self-image)? Our free will allows us to make this choice. In every moment, free will is present in how we create and experience life. We are either conscious, i.e., aware of what is directing our choices and actions or not. If we are conscious of the values, beliefs and assumptions that direct our thoughts, then we truly are exercising free will.

Free will is about choosing to live with love. Ego is a part of our physical experience and so is encompassed by our divinity. The primary choice is: Do we identify with and live solely from ego or do we live our divinity with ego being part of our physical body? Do we act from Source and the Truth that our essence is love? This is self-transcendence, the transcendence of ego. And this brings freedom, freedom from the limitations of ego, so we experience the depth and wholeness of our true nature. It is the liberation of our soul. The truth of who we are really does set us free.

Summary of Our Primary Choice

	Ego	Divinity
Based in	Fear	Love
Believe we are	Separate	One
Life experience	Protect self-image	Connection with others Joy in uniqueness and coming home

This is a universe of infinite possibilities that we can choose from. As a creator, everything in the universe, all possible experiences are within each of us to bring or manifest into physical reality by our choices. One aspect of manifestation is attraction. The Law of Attraction is simply that like attracts like. What we attract into our lives is based on our *own* thoughts, beliefs and assumptions. Everything, including thought, is energy at differing levels of vibration. These vibrations attract other energy of similar vibrations. When we believe in something, we set up a vibration and direct our energy toward it, creating what we experience. Thoughts with emotion set up a vibration that attracts, bringing about change. Thoughts without emotion maintain the status quo.

Through our thoughts, beliefs and assumptions, whether conscious or not, we create our experience and bring energy into matter, which becomes our reality. In essence, beliefs charged with our emotions direct energy towards something. Emotions are energy in motion, a consciousness of feelings from the heart that amplify the vibration of thoughts. Love-based emotions are from

Source, fear-based emotions are from ego. Fear-based emotions cause contraction or constriction in the flow of love in our lives. Why do we choose to close what is natural to us? Let love flow! Love-based emotions tell us when we are aligned with Spirit's will for us. Where we direct our energy – our emotions – will increase or expand our experience of that emotion. Fear brings more fear. Love brings more love.

While we share experiences, our reality is unique to each of us. Let me repeat this: We share experiences but our reality is unique because our thoughts that created the experience and shape our perceptions of it are unique. From the viewpoint of ego or separation, it might be said that there is no one reality. When my husband tells me that I am "out of touch with reality," I am. I do not and cannot know *his* reality. At the same time, I am very much in touch with *my* reality. These separate realities that we create are from ego. Nothing in our experiences has meaning except the meaning that we give it. As the Buddha said, "Our life is shaped by our mind; we become what we think."

There is only one ultimate reality, that of Spirit: oneness, uniqueness, free will and love. Every object and being is divine. We pretend and tell ourselves otherwise, so this is not what we think we see on the physical plane. No matter what we or someone else chooses, it is of Source because we are never separate. In the moment we may forget that we are one with Spirit, but we always are in oneness, with our uniqueness and free will. If we kill another, it is because we have chosen to forget our divinity and our oneness.

Dynamics of Love and Relationship

What is love? Love is any energy that enhances and expands life. It is life-giving, unconditionally accepting that each of us and all of creation is of Source. Love in action is compassion, acknowledging that we are one. It is acceptance, non-judgment, forgiveness and wisdom. It is acknowledging that we have a free will to make our own choices and experiences. Following a path of love brings us home to Spirit.

Conversely, fear is the absence of love. It is an energy that causes contraction or suppression of the full experience of life. This usually will be expressed as some kind of control, limitation or coercion of your own or another's free will. Fear also seeks to deny our oneness and uniqueness. Again, our oneness is the basis of the teaching, "Do unto others what you would have them do to you." What you do to others, you do to yourself and what you do to yourself, you do to others. The question is: Is this something that you would do to yourself or would want to have done to you?

There is a related principle that I will call the "Rule of Relationship and Reciprocity." It is captured by the statement, "you reap what you sow." Relationships are dynamic such that what you give, you receive – respect brings respect, violence brings violence, trust brings trust, peace within self brings peace to the world. We gain power, which is love, by giving it, allowing others the sanctity of their free will. Everything that we think, say or do has consequences, which will come back to us in our lifetime. This is what Buddhists call "karma."

We cannot give to others what we do not have ourselves, so giving to self is always first. In addition, our relationships with others are *always* direct reflections of aspects of our relationship with our essence, with Spirit. All relationships are dynamic, that is, active and changing with a purpose. All relationships are sacred. All relationships enable us to experience our humanness. It is through our relationships with others that we can choose to experience our oneness, uniqueness and free will. It is only in relationship that we experience wholeness and it is only in wholeness that we can be in true relationship. The only way we can know our divine selves is in relationship, in interaction with others.

The paradox is this: Only by going *inside of ourselves* to fully connect to Source can we be fully present in our relationships with *others*. Presence is the attunement with our uniqueness, our oneness and our free will. It creates a signature energy that no one else possesses. When fully present, we are connected to our spiritual core. This enables others to connect to their spiritual core and Spirit is present with us in the relationship.

If we feel disrespected by others, it is because we don't truly respect ourselves as divine beings, therefore we are not able to give respect. If we don't trust our divine nature, we will not be able to give trust and therefore will not be trusted by others. Our relationships with others are our greatest teachers and healers.

Self-love is first. We cannot love others unless we love ourselves. Self-love is the unconditional acceptance of all our experiences and full integration of our body, mind, emotions and spirit.

When we love ourselves, we set up the vibration of love, attracting more love into our lives. When we dislike, disown or deny part of ourselves, we establish this vibrational frequency in ourselves, attracting more of what we don't like or disown into our lives. This is summarized by the statement, "What we resist, persists." This means that what we disown or deny in ourselves, will keep showing up in our lives until we accept it as part of us and our life experience. By our resistance, we are actually focusing energy on it and attracting it into our life. Spirit is showing us what we need to heal, guiding our path towards wholeness. Our goal is to return to Source.

A similar statement, "If you spot it, you got it," means that if we see something in another that irritates us or that we admire, it is because it is a part of us. We will not have an emotional reaction unless we have the characteristic within us, which we either reject or accept. Rejection results in irritation; acceptance results in admiration.

Fear of anyone or anything is a belief in that person or object, so when we fear something, we attract it into our lives. You might say, "Why is this?" Again, our thoughts and beliefs set up a vibration that directs or pulls energy toward something. By attracting something we fear into our life, it is Spirit's way of giving us the opportunity to consciously choose love rather than fear. If you truly desire something that is based in love, and it is not part of your current reality, it is because it is being prevented by thoughts that counter the desire. If you want to know both your conscious and unconscious thoughts and beliefs, just look around you. Consciousness is simply awareness; unconsciousness is simply lack of awareness. If your experiences are "negative," it is because your thoughts and beliefs are "negative." We can just as easily believe in and direct our energy toward something positive.

Fearlessness is the absence of fear. It is based in trust and faith in our connection to Spirit. Courage is acknowledging our fears and moving forward or acting from love anyway. Without fear, we are set free from having a constrained life. We are liberated from ego to live a life consistent with our divine nature. Fearlessness brings complete freedom.

Gratitude for what we have and desire is a powerful attractor because it is the acknowledgement that our desires are already so. It is the appreciation of the love that is ever present. Everything, "good" or "bad," is an expression of Spirit. We can choose to be grateful for a "bad" experience because of the lesson it gives us. Through this learning we know to choose differently next time.

Living in the present moment means that we choose to be free of past thoughts, beliefs, emotions and experiences so that we don't project and manifest them into our future. It is an openness to experience life in a new way, not tied to our past. It is the choice that comes from the alignment of our body, mind, emotions and spirit in the now. It is living as an expression of love.

Self-awareness and self-mastery enables living in the present moment. Self-mastery is complete awareness of ourselves, our thoughts, emotions, body and spirit, so that we can consciously choose our actions. Mastery is *critical* for leaders so that we don't project our beliefs and emotions onto others' experience. We take responsibility for our thoughts and choices and enable others to do the same, respecting their uniqueness and free will.

The nature of the human experience is change; it is the nature of life to change and grow. When we are not influenced by the ups and downs of change and choose to be present, joy is our internal state of consciousness. We can be joyful – in a state of joy – for each and every experience in our lives and with the innocence of a child.

A discussion of the nature of life would not be complete without a mention of the nature of death. Death is the transition back to Source, a return to our divine essence. It is merely a release of the physical body. We leave the illusion of separation and return to oneness. Death can be thought of as the ultimate act of surrender, of choosing to complete our journey and fully return to love.

FORGIVENESS AND NON-JUDGMENT

Forgiveness is acknowledging that we sometimes forget that our essence is love, that we are one. We use free will to protect our ego, our self-image, and forget our own true divine nature of love. In the moment, we both just forgot who we really are! We chose fear rather than love and FEAR is False Expectations Appearing Real. When we are in fear of anyone or anything, we are denying their divine nature as part of Spirit. With forgiveness, we give back and acknowledge that our essence is love.

The primary forgiveness is self-forgiveness, acknowledging that we acted in ignorance of our divinity and interconnectedness. You cannot give to others what you do not have. When you are angry with someone, if you first forgive yourself for being angry, then you can forgive them for what they did from your perspective. When we forgive ourselves, everyone else is forgiven as well! The greatest shift of awareness in forgiveness comes not from giving back essence, but rather from being grateful for the experience. Each experience of forgiveness is a reminder to nudge us closer to living who we are and to being aware of our connection to Source. Forgiveness opens the heart to love.

Judgment is part of a dualistic or polar view of reality that we create from the illusion of separation from each other and Source. I am not talking about cognitive judgment, making a decision or choice. Judgment in the context of this book is having an *opinion* about a person, event or object, e.g., good/bad, right/wrong, pretty/ugly. It is our ego that has a need to judge to protect our image of who we think we are. Judgment is the need to control. It includes an expectation of our self or others which denies our uniqueness and free will. Our actions do not require judgment, guilt or shame. We act either with or without awareness of Spirit. Because of our oneness, when we judge another, we ultimately judge ourselves. "Let he who is without fault cast the first stone."

Non-judgment is witnessing or holding up a mirror without opinion, describing what you see or experience.

When we do not judge ourselves, we have no need to forgive ourselves or others.

Related to judgment is attachment, which is a desire to control another or an outcome. Detachment is relinquishing control because we respect each other's uniqueness and free will; it is not indifference. With loving detachment we support another's choice and path.

To relate these concepts back to business, can you imagine a business where our management practices do not judge? What would performance management look like? How would we allocate compensation and rewards? How many times have we embedded judgment and control into our practices without even considering what we are doing? What about position and power? Since we are all divine, we are all equal. We do have different purposes to fulfill and a path that is ours alone, but we *are equals*. When leaders maintain a loving detachment, they enable others' uniqueness and free will.

Serving Life means that we acknowledge and nurture our divine nature in all that we do. This service includes business, which is a primary means to convey the flow of divine love and abundance (e.g., employee prosperity, business growth, profitability and shareholder value). We, as co-creators, as leaders, can foster this flow or stop it in its tracks. Leadership that serves life is generative, and through our business life we *can* choose to serve all of life: our oneness, our uniqueness and our free will.

Oneness. Uniqueness. Free will. Three simple truths.

May there be peace within you today.

May you trust your highest power that you are exactly where you are meant to be.

May you not forget the infinite possibilities that are born of faith.

May you use those gifts that you have received, and pass on the love that has been given to you.

May you be content knowing you are a child of God.

Let this presence settle into your bones, and allow your soul the freedom to sing, dance, and to bask in the sun; it is there for each and every one of you.

Unknown

CHAPTER REFLECTIONS

What was your "ah-ha" moment? What did you read that validates or changes how you think about creation, reality and who you are?

What are you going to do differently or what actions are you going to take as a result of these insights?

3

OUR DIVINITY IS HARDWIRED INTO OUR HUMANITY

In my heart, I receive will, wisdom and truth from Source.
Through love, power and creativity, I bring the divine into manifest,
physical form.

Lucira

As in the last chapter, I am going to be giving you just a high level summary. I do not do justice to the elegance of our human body. The best I can do is to highlight key points to help you to "connect the dots" of how our divinity is hardwired into our humanity.

We are truly remarkable beings. We are part of Source and we have the same image and likeness. This means we are hardwired (physiologically) and have the software (energy structures and psychological needs) for our divine nature. We are free to turn this hardware and software on or off as we choose. We can build the hardware and program the software any way we want, or we can allow others to program us. We are structured to interpret and act in the world with Spirit through our physical bodies.

Again, everything is energy, including our thoughts. Some energy (vibration) is denser than others (hence we can see it). We are learning from quantum physics that thoughts create matter. So, let's start with the brain.

In the chart on the next page, I have related our divine nature with our brain structure and innate psychological needs, derived from the work motivation literature from business and psychology.

BRAIN PHYSIOLOGY

Our prefrontal lobes connect our emotions, values and goals. They are future-oriented. The limbic system responds to emotions. It is the part of the brain that wants to interact and bond. Interestingly, the limbic is the part of the brain that responds automatically or reactively through instinct or training. Our natural or instinctual state is to want to connect with others; we learn and condition ourselves for competition and separation. For many, the Internet is addictive because it enables us to connect and experience our oneness.

The neo-cortex is where we process experience and learning, and it is proactive. It is the source of our creativity and it enjoys novelty. The right hemisphere processes our intuition, creativity, symbolic and relational thinking. The left hemisphere is our reasoning center for logical, linear, sequential thinking.

ALIGNMENT AMONG OUR DIVINE NATURE, BRAIN PHYSIOLOGY AND PSYCHOLOGICAL NEEDS

Divine Nature	Brain Physiology	Function	Psychological Needs
Oneness	Limbic System	Respond to emotions; interact & bond	Connection & Participation – To be part of something larger than ourselves
Uniqueness	Pre-frontal Lobes	Future oriented; connect our emotions, values & goals	Purpose & Meaning – To bring value & benefit to others; to enhance life
Free Will	Integration of entire brain	Connect body, mind, emotions and spirit for action	Self-determination & Choice – To choose our life experiences
Return to Source	Neo-cortex	Process experience & learning	Growth & Creativity – To expand who we know ourselves to be
Unconditional, Selfless Love	Brain stem	Gatekeeper to cortical or limbic response; access to higher processing	Respect, Acceptance & Appreciation – To be appreciated for our uniqueness and be loved

Our brain stem and the Reticular Activating System are the gatekeepers. They control whether we have a cortical or limbic response. The brain stem can also respond on its own (fight, flight or freeze) without accessing our "higher" brain centers. Its purpose is protection and survival, so when we experience safety, familiarity and consistency, the brain stem "opens" access to our higher processing.

The complete integration of our brain and nervous system with the heart is the physiological structure of our divinity (see Heartmath's research on the power of the heart). Spirit guides us through our emotions and intuition. The part(s) of the brain that we access determines how we choose to respond to an experience. For example, if we are in fear, initially we do not have full access beyond the brain stem. However, we can choose to override the immediate fight, flight or freeze response and access more conscious thought, or we can respond from the brain stem. How many times do you feel you are interacting with someone who is either striking at you or running away? They are operating primarily from their brain stem out of fear. When we choose to stay in fear we literally have limited access to our "higher" brain centers – they are shut down.

PSYCHOLOGICAL NEEDS

The literature on human motivation from research in work settings shows that we have five major psychological needs (the detail of the research is available from the author on request). These needs correspond with our brain physiology (again, see chart on Page 31) and they help guide our healing and return to Source:

- Purpose and meaning: To bring value and be of benefit to others; to enhance life.
- Growth and development: To expand who we know ourselves to be.
- Connection and participation: To be part of something larger than ourselves.
- Respect: To be appreciated for our uniqueness and be loved.
- Self-determination and choice: To choose our life experiences.

These "needs" can be thought of as part of our guidance system so that we unite with Source. They are part of our "software."

ENERGY CENTERS

Our energy centers, or chakras, are also part of our "software" and provide our direct connection to Source. These are centers of electromagnetic energy that communicate and connect to our bodies through our endocrine glands and major nerve ganglia throughout our body. The chakras function as receptors, assimilators and transmitters of life energy. They influence the endocrine system to communicate with different parts of our body through the release of hormones.

Together the Crown Chakra (Will), the Third Eye (Wisdom) and the Throat Chakra (Truth) are the Divine or Sacred Masculine centers, representing "father." We tap into our wisdom when we integrate thoughts from our prefrontal lobes with both of our right and left hemispheres of our neo-cortex.

CORRESPONDENCE BETWEEN THE CHAKRAS AND THE ENDOCRINE SYSTEM

Chakra Centers	Endocrine Glands
CROWN – Divine will, connection to Source	Pineal
THIRD EYE – Clear sight, intuition, wisdom	Pituitary
THROAT – Truth, surrender personal will to the will of the divine	Thyroid/Parathyroid
HEART – Love, compassion forgiveness, divine power	Thymus
SOLAR PLEXUS – Personal power, self-esteem, ego, honor self	Pancreas
SECOND CHAKRA – Creativity, self-worth, confidence, emotions, honor others	Ovaries/Gonads
ROOT – Connection to the world, material world, foundation, manifestation	Adrenals

The Heart Chakra, as the Divine or Sacred Feminine center, represents "mother." It receives will from Source and through love brings will into physical form. We are creating all the time either from ego or Source. The love of the heart is the great transformer that enables and brings the will of Source to humanity. It is *only through love that the will of Spirit* is made physical. Our heart provides the energy of our emotions and is the power that enables thought to come into being.

The Solar Plexus Chakra (Personal Power), the Second Chakra (Creation) and Root Chakra (Manifestation) enable divine will to become physical matter or experience. So, the vertical axis of our physical body connects us to the will of Spirit which we then bring to the physical plane.

Our chakras and our intuition are our connection to Spirit. Our physical body is our connection with the world, our human experience. For example, when we stand straight with our arms extended, we physically form a cross, which is one symbol of our divinity and our humanity. The Trinity and making the Sign of the Cross in the Catholic tradition also exemplify our divinity: Father (oneness), Son (uniqueness) and Spirit (free will). Another physical reminder of our divinity is when we extend our arms and spread our legs and connect the major points, creating the Star of David. This is another symbol of the integration of our humanity with our divinity.

OUR HUMANITY, OUR DIVINITY

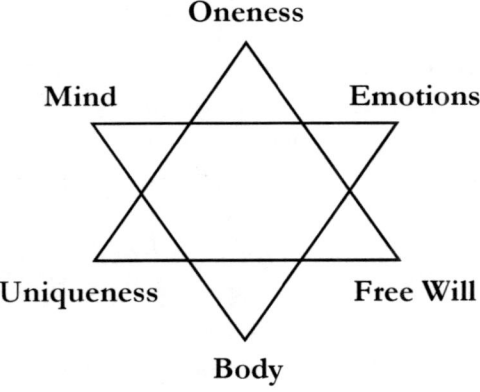

The left side of our physical body is considered our connection to the feminine through which we receive the gifts of the world. It is governed by the right side of our brain. The right side of our physical body is considered the masculine through which we give our gifts to the world. It is governed by the left side of our brain. What we consider traditionally feminine qualities are those qualities that are based in love and are focused on relationships and nurturing. In business, we frequently call these "soft skills." Traditional male qualities are those of logical thought, direct action and "defense" or "protection." We are meant to integrate the feminine and the masculine, to both nurture and defend life, love and our divinity. The masculine logic of the left hemisphere helps to translate the feminine, intuitive symbols of the right hemisphere, so that we can "hear" on the physical plane what Spirit is saying to us. The masculine provides structure for experience, the feminine. In business we create structures that either cause contraction or expansion.

Going back to the Rule of Relationship and Reciprocity, the quality of our relationship with both the Divine Masculine and the Divine Feminine comprise our relationship to Source. Our experience of our mother will show us our relationship with the Divine Feminine; our experience of our father will show us our relationship with the Divine Masculine. In other words, our relationships with our parents can show us what we need to heal to be able to return to Source. These are generally "big" things, e.g., a belief in (fear of) betrayal and abandonment. Again, we can choose to be either conscious or unconscious of our experiences with our parents. When we are conscious of our experiences with our parents, we know how we can strengthen our connection to Spirit. If we experienced unconditional love from our parents, we are blessed with the foundation of a strong relationship with Spirit.

Growing Home to Source

When we look at human development models, such as Maslow's Hierarchy of Needs or Clare Graves' model on the development of human values, Spiral Dynamics, we can see a relationship between how we develop and mature and open our chakras, our energy centers (see chart, Page 39). In other words, models of human development implicitly address our energy centers. Both models explicitly acknowledge that our development is not a linear process. Rather, we will exhibit multiple stages at any one point in time as we grow into subsequent stages. So, too, at different times in our development and in life in general, we are more or less open to each of our energy centers.

Spiral Dynamics is interesting in its application to organizations (and any collective, including nations) because it describes the prevailing value set, which is what really matters and dictates how things get done. It essentially describes the culture. For example, the current culture and values of the United States and our businesses are predominantly Red, Blue and Orange with Green emerging (see chart on Page 39). Both Afghanistan and Iraq are examples of the struggle to move from Red to Blue.

Ken Wilbur's writing about Spiral Dynamics in *A Theory of Everything* helped me to appreciate that if someone is at one level of beliefs in the Spiral, they literally cannot "see" or understand the perspective of the "higher" levels. As we develop and progress up the Spiral, we integrate the lessons of our experience from the levels below. In other words, if we are thinking and acting from primarily Green values, we have already experienced and integrated Red, Blue and Orange. If we are predominantly at Blue in our development, Green values make absolutely no sense to us.

I would like to pause and ask you to think about: What is your own predominant value set? What is the predominant value set of your business?

Please note that while the charts in this chapter look linear, the relationships among the concepts are not. Rather, they are highly interdependent and integrated.

Here are a few thoughts to consider. At one point, I read that the field of psychology emerged when science split from religion (mystical aspects of life) and split our physical being from our souls. So, in essence, the purpose of psychology is to reunite us with our soul. What if psychology became the "science" of soul reclamation and healing? What would be the focus of Industrial-Organizational Psychology (the basis of my education) which has guided our leadership and management practices since World War II?

COMPARISON OF CHAKRA ENERGY CENTERS WITH THE HUMAN DEVELOPMENT MODELS OF MASLOW'S HIERARCHY OF NEEDS AND CLARE GRAVES' SPIRAL DYNAMICS

Maslow	Chakras	Spiral Dynamics
SELF-TRANSCENDENCE – Purpose, wholeness and integration	CROWN – Divine will, connection to Source	CORAL – Enlightened, works to bring out inherent potential of others
	THIRD EYE – Clear sight, intuition, wisdom	TURQUOISE – Wholeness of existence, wisdom, compassion, integrated planet
SELF-ACTUALIZATION – Make most of unique abilities, reach one's fullest potential	THROAT – Truth, surrender personal will to the divine	YELLOW – Live fully and responsibly, integrated self, personal self-mastery
ESTEEM – Confidence, achievement, respect of self and others	HEART – Love, compassion, forgiveness, divine power	GREEN – Caring dimensions of community, equality, liberty
LOVE/BELONGING – Family, friendship, intimacy	SOLAR PLEXUS – Personal power, self-esteem, ego, honor self	ORANGE – Enterprising self interest, success driven
SAFETY – Security of body, family, health, resources	SECOND – Creativity, self-worth, confidence, emotions, honor others	BLUE – Ordered existence, rules, dualistic, authoritarian RED – Survival of the strongest, power driven, egocentric PURPLE – Social, honor family, seek harmony
PHYSICAL – Breathing, food water, sleep, shelter	ROOT – Connection to the world, material world, foundation, manifestation	BEIGE – Survival, being human, shelter, safety

When we live consciously and come from a place of complete integrity (i.e., the integration of body, mind, emotions and spirit) this wholeness enacts our divinity. Said another way, when we honor our humanity, we honor our divinity. The two are inseparable. Therefore, when we as leaders, through our business and organizational practices, honor our humanness, we honor our divine nature. Organizational effectiveness practices are actually human effectiveness practices. Let's make business a place of fun and play with our divinity!

May the light at the core of your being illuminate the world.

Kate Nowak

CHAPTER REFLECTIONS

What was your "ah-ha" moment? What did you read that validates or changes how you think about our physical and divine natures?

What are you going to do differently or what actions are you going to take as a result of these insights?

4

IF ALL THIS IS TRUE, WHY THE STATE OF THE WORLD?

Humanity has just crossed the most important threshold we have ever crossed or will ever cross. We have enough for everyone to have a healthy and productive life.

Buckminster Fuller

Buckminster Fuller made this observation in the 1970s. Think about it. This was 30 years ago. Look around. Everywhere you look we have much conflict, violence and poverty. We live in a world filled with abundance. So, why all the fear and competition? We believe in scarcity. Conflict and violence emerge when we focus on our ego, protecting our self-image, and defending our beliefs rather than loving each other.

David Hawkins makes a comparison of Power versus Force. True power is from within; it is from Spirit as love. Force is external; it is imposed. Many people in supposedly powerful roles today are not true leaders. They use external force and not their internal power of love. They have chosen fear and cut themselves off from Source and their divine nature and seek to do the same to others. They are acting from ego, using force to control and therefore not enabling the divine empowerment of all. They are denying the truth of our oneness and unity, our uniqueness and our free will.

Their words and actions are violent, violence being anything that denies the light and love of another. Above all they seek control and contraction of others to feed the illusion of their power. They are operating from fear and seek to create fear in others. Fear is a powerful motivator bringing an instinctual contraction of fight, flight or freeze. Judgment brings fear and induces contraction, limiting others' contribution and ability to connect. In fear, we act from the brain stem, seeking protection and survival.

War is actually a physical manifestation of the metaphor for the internal battles we wage by our rejection of our divine nature. Again, all relationships are about our relationship with Source within. When we wage war with another it is because we reject the truth of our being. Waging war in the name of Spirit is never justified. Love doesn't create or engage in war. Source does not fight or kill another because everyone and everything is part of Source. Love has no enemies.

Our real "enemies" are our own beliefs that deny our essence. It is ego that says we are not one with others and they are not divine. We are called to take responsibility for our actions and our contribution to the situation. We can choose to seek common ground and look for what connects us, our oneness.

Through the electoral process in democracies, we can choose leaders who reflect our collective shadow and fears. Or, we can choose leaders who reflect our belief that we are indeed divine and that the greatest power is love. No one can take our power from us. When we allow others to have power over us, it is because we have chosen to give it to them. When we choose to give our power over to another, we essentially deny our divinity.

The United States Declaration of Independence was divinely inspired: "We hold these truths to be self-evident, that all men are created equal, that they are endowed by their Creator with certain unalienable Rights that among these are Life (oneness), Liberty (free will) and the pursuit of Happiness (uniqueness)." Let us reclaim our divine heritage, the founding principles of life: Unity/Oneness, Uniqueness and Free Will.

Every country has its role in humanity's return to Source. The spiritual leader Sai Maa Lakshmi Devi teaches that "U.S.A." stands for "Ultimate Self Awareness." The role and gift of the United States is to bring this Awareness to the world. Our freedoms, our liberties, give us the opportunity to choose to experience who we really are, the ultimate awareness of self as divine.

Changing the world is not an impossible task. The

community service organization Rotary International has a Four Way Test that guides their actions:

♦ Is it the truth?
♦ Is it fair to all concerned?
♦ Will it build goodwill and better friendship (relationships)?
♦ Will it be beneficial to all concerned?

Imagine the quality of life we all would have if this were an integral part of government and business.

Love is always the answer. And, as Thaddeus Golas wrote in his classic, *The Lazy Man's Guide to Enlightenment,* when others act in ways that are not loving, they are endeavoring to bring your energy down to match the level of their energy. Love them even more.

Let there be peace on earth and let it begin with me.

Divine Spirit, through our collective essence of Love, we and all people manifest you in this world. As co-creators, thank you for helping us to be the peace we desire. We choose to bring the Love who we are and so bring peace, through whatever purpose we have or role we play with our families and friends, at our workplace or in our business interactions. In this way, we change the world.

May we seek deep understanding of those different from us to foster our compassion and acceptance. May all of our beliefs, thoughts and actions be based in and manifest your unconditional Love. It is so.

Lucira

CHAPTER REFLECTIONS

What was your "ah-ha" moment? What did you read that validates or changes how you think about what we see in the world around us?

What are you going to do differently or what actions are you going to take as a result of these insights?

5

A GRAND POSSIBILITY: BUSINESS LEADERS AS MIDWIVES WHO BIRTH A NEW WORLD

Transformation occurs because we invite others into a different conversation.

Diana Whitney

You are probably wondering why I chose the word "midwife" for the title of this chapter. Midwife means "someone or something that helps to create or produce something new." In this context, true leaders are midwives.

So how can we apply the Universal Principles to business or organizations? If you are a business executive, this chapter will begin to give you some ideas on how the principles translate into your leadership. If you are not an executive, perhaps this will give you ideas on how you can lead from where you are. Whether or not you are in a business leadership role per se, you can be a leader in changing the world.

In today's world, the prevalent assumption is that the purpose of business is to make money, to maximize profits and shareholder value. This belief tends to focus activities on competition for the limited financial resources of customers and investors, with winners and losers in a zero-sum game. The concept of limited resources generally creates a fear of loss, which leads to the need to control. In turn, the need to control often results in authoritarian actions, with power garnered by hierarchical position, and with management-employee interactions characterized by patriarchy and dependence.

Motivation is believed to come from external sources, giving managers another reason to control. Measures which focus on outputs and outcomes are generally imposed, and people are judged against them, leading to governance of others through fear. People gauge their value based on whether they are approved of by others. Productivity and efficiency are the presumed direct causes of financial gain. Work is broken into efficient parts and employees are seen as parts of a machine and as expenses (costs) to be managed. The presumed need for efficiency results in people being treated as replaceable parts. This is one reason why when a company announces layoffs in the interest of expense management, the stock price goes up.

Change is imposed, controlled, managed. Managers seek to control the whole by breaking it apart and working with the fragments.

Reflect for a moment. What do I believe is the purpose of business? What do I believe creates business success?

ENERGY OF BUSINESS SUCCESS

Business management practices since the 1950s (e.g., Participative Management, Empowerment, Vision/Values and Learning Organizations) do not identify the underlying cause as to why they improve work performance. Simply put, these practices have a direct effect on performance and profitability because they nurture an aspect of our divinity. Until a few brave souls began using the "S" word (Spirituality) in business, we just kept tap dancing around this big elephant in the room without naming it. Radical as it may seem, nurturing our divinity is the *root cause* of business success.

A conversation with a close friend put the importance of root cause into perspective. Business is about people producing something or providing a service for the good of others. A company's performance cannot be separated from its people. Business *is* its people. Somehow we forget this and don't understand why we are choosing to act the way we do or to put something into practice. Our actions and behaviors are reinforced by the systems that we create, with or without thought of our human essence. In the end, without thinking about *why* we are doing something in our business lives, we lose our human essence. It's not about the practice per se; it's *why* we do the practice that is important.

Again, we have innate needs for purposeful work with the

opportunity to serve, the opportunity to express ourselves and make our own choices to determine the course of our lives. This is our humanness. It is our humanness that motivates us and brings us to high performance. As you can see from the model on the next page, managing companies using our humanness as the guide to business practices leads to financial success.

This chart is an adaptation of the Service-Profit Chain published in several articles during the 1990s in the *Harvard Business Review*. Simply stated, is says that the marketplace energy directs the Foundation of the business, which directs the Operational Practices of the business. Together, the Foundation and Operational Practices create an environment and energy that guides employee behavior. How employees act, creates the customer experience, which increases or decreases profitability. The key point of the chart is to base the Foundation and Operational Practices in Universal Principles. They are the *why* and provide guidance to leaders in their actions.

Bottom line: Business leadership based in Universal Principles creates financial abundance.

The energy that creates business success, manifested through the divine principles that support our humanness, is significantly different than when the purpose of business is profit. Historically, beginning in the 1800s, the original intent and purpose of corporations was to serve and benefit others, both customers and employees. From this perspective, they used practices based on cooperation

ENERGY OF BUSINESS SUCCESS

Marketplace Opportunities Customer Requirements & Expectations	Shareholders INVEST in company's ability to create value		Employees CREATE value	Customers PURCHASE value	Superior Growth, Profitability & Shareholder Value
	Foundation	Operational Practices	Employee	Customer	
	• Purpose • Strategy / Branding • Values • Organization Design • Governance	• Communication • Planning & Monitoring • Performance & Contribution Enhancement • Shared Rewards • Engagement & Development	• Wholeness • Commitment • Performance Quality / service Productivity Innovation	• Acquisition • Satisfaction • Retention	

• Oneness: Connection, Participation, Inclusion, Equality
• Uniqueness: Purpose & Meaning
• Free will: Self-determination & Choice
• Actualization: Growth & Development
• Selfless Love, Compassion & Non-judgment: Respect, Acceptance & Appreciation

Leadership in Service to Life creates the Environment from the Principles that Affirm Our Humanness and Divinity resulting in Abundance for all

and collaboration (vs. competition) to serve the common good. Profit is still important as an *outcome*, but it is not the *purpose*.

WHAT IS LEADERSHIP?

Peter Drucker said leaders enable the "alignment of strengths so that 'weaknesses' are irrelevant." Leaders' work is to foster each individual's unique purpose and contribution (their unique gift of love from Spirit) to be in alignment with the purpose of the organization, the collective. Leaders who serve life recognize the divinity in everyone. Leaders who serve life create an environment from the principles that affirm our humanness and our divinity, resulting in abundance for all. Practices based in oneness, uniqueness, and free will enhance our human capabilities and optimize individual and collective contributions. This creates breakthrough results because we access and amplify each individual's limitless potential to create.

More than anything, leadership is a state of being.
True leaders have mastered wholeness of body, mind, emotions and spirit and are living with full consciousness. Leadership starts with who you are, your state of being, and moves to what you do, your actions. These actions are always within the context of the external and internal environment. It is in who we are and how we show up that we, as leaders, create a field of resonance, vibrational energy that will attract and enable others to live their wholeness. As Michael Ray says in his book, *The Highest Goal*, resonance is catalytic. "It causes reactions without

being diminished. It is endlessly generative," able to create something new.

In their book, *Geeks and Geezers*, Warren Bennis and Robert Thomas offer four leadership characteristics that transcend eras, generations and cultures (their labels are used below). In *Building the Bridge as You Walk on It*, Robert Quinn talks about the Fundamental State of Leadership, which contains similar concepts. Combining these models captures the essence of leadership and reflects a state of internal being that is generative and life-supporting for others, respecting oneness, uniqueness and free will.

ADAPTIVE CAPACITY

Am I externally open? This is the ability to process experiences, find their meaning and integrate them into one's life. It means transcendence, going beyond limits and adversity. It means looking for wisdom from experience, including insights for learning how we learn. It includes using context to create connections and interaction, weighing factors ranging from how very different groups will interpret gestures, to being able to put a situation in perspective. It is learning while doing in order to achieve mastery. It is finding or making new rules rather than being constrained by existing "fixed" rules.

ENGAGE OTHERS THROUGH SHARED MEANING

Am I other focused? This is the capacity to abandon one's ego and listen to others. It means helping others surface their ideas and talents and being attuned to the needs of others. It is enrolling other people in a dream, finding opportunities, and giving appreciation instead of finding fault. It is learning and teaching through shared stories. It is encouraging dissent to find common ground. It is committing to the collective good.

VOICE

Am I internally directed? This is authenticity, clarifying one's core values and speaking and acting from what one stands for. It is fidelity in presenting oneself, living what one believes. It is choosing words carefully, testing oneself before testing others. It is coming from a place of deep self-reflection, questioning who you are and what matters to you. It is examining values and surfacing assumptions to strengthen a sense of purpose, and helping others to do the same.

INTEGRITY

Am I results centered? This is balancing ambition (desire to lead), technical competence and moral compass (or absolutes of your values). It is moving toward possibilities that don't yet exist. It is wholeness, the full and conscious integration of body, mind, emotions and spirit.

Leaders appreciate the difference between deep structure and surface features, between essence and superficiality. Rather than focusing on the surface, what we see, leaders focus on the cause, the essence of who we are. Leaders know we are one and seek to foster our connection. They appreciate each person's uniqueness and enable us to use our gifts. They respect each person's free will and provide opportunities for true choice.

ORGANIZATIONAL CHANGE

In closing this chapter, I'd like to offer just a few observations about organizational change. First, there is really no such thing as "organizational change" as we currently think about it. All change is self-change, and we each have to choose to change. Change is individual, so "organizational change" really means focus on fostering individual change. "Change management" is an oxymoron because we cannot control whether others choose to change. The only person we can change is ourselves. When we try to impose or "get" others to change, we deny their free will. When we change as leaders and personally live and lead differently, we invite others to do the same. We transform others only by transforming ourselves. This is our power as leaders: We enable others' Adaptive Capacity, Shared Meaning, Voice and Integrity.

Leading change is about engaging others in co-creation. We can nurture change through clarity, consistency of words and actions and by enabling commitment through choice. In consciously working with the Law of Attraction, we establish thoughts, emotions and actions which create the energetic vibration that brings what we desire into being.

Leaders, at any level, have a key responsibility in transformation and change, that of self-awareness. When we are self-aware, we can ensure that we don't project our own "stuff," our thoughts, beliefs and assumptions, onto others. If we project our own perceptions into the environment, we can't hold the space for others to see and experience who they really are. We limit their ability to grow and create.

Organizational change is collective manifestation. It is a dynamic, interdependent process. It is about a shared mindset. It is about thoughts, beliefs and emotions driving actions toward a common purpose and goal. It is about learning and growth. It is about uniqueness and integrity. We cannot make choices for others. For organizational change to occur, the free will of others requires that they make their own choice to share our desires. When we negate others' free will by excluding their participation in the change process, we close their hearts and stop the co-creation.

Oneness. Uniqueness. Free will. Three simple truths.

I lead by word and deed simply because I am here doing what I do.

The power for authentic leadership is not found in external arrangements but in the human heart. Authentic leaders in every setting aim at liberating the heart, their own and others', so that its power can liberate the world.... External reality does not impinge upon us as an ultimate constraint: If we who are privileged find ourselves confined, it is only because we have conspired in our own imprisonment... we make the world what it is by projecting our spirit on it, for better or for worse. If our institutions are rigid, it is because our hearts fear change; if they set us in mindless competition with each other, it is because we value victory above all else; if they are heedless of human well-being, it because something in us is heartless as well.

We all can make choices about what we are going to project, and with those choices we help grow the world that is. Consciousness precedes being: consciousness, yours and mine, can form, deform or reform our world. Our complicity in world-making is a source of awesome and sometimes painful responsibility — and a source of profound hope for change. It is the ground of our common call to leadership, the truth that makes leaders of us all.

Let Your Life Speak
Parker Palmer

CHAPTER REFLECTIONS

What was your "ah-ha" moment? What did you read that validates or changes how you think about leadership and business?

What are you going to do differently or what actions are you going to take as a result of these insights?

6

ORDER FROM CHAOS: ORGANIZATIONAL PRACTICES

Love is both the context for and structure within all aspects of creation and life. Love brings order to chaos.

Lucira

Organizations are a collective of individuals, and often we experience them as chaotic. Business and organizational leaders have the opportunity to create new "rules," principles by which we enable others to actualize their divine nature. Based in universal laws, these principles will nurture, enhance life, and create expansion in all ways, including business growth and profitability.

Conventional business practices stifle growth. And "best practices" really don't exist, because the context of, and the people in, each business are different. We know the potential of our people and, as leaders, desire to liberate this power and enable each individual to contribute to their fullest. Our conflict is that we want to unleash this power and, at the same time, we fear it. We fear that if we don't establish boundaries we will have chaos or worse. So, many of our organizational practices "prescribe" behaviors – what we want people to do and how we want them to do it. These externally imposed controls and their accompanying judgments cause contraction. They are based in and cause fear, essentially saying, "We don't fully accept your uniqueness and free will." We experience practices that diminish who we are at our essence and we want to cry out:

♦ I am not my personality. I am not my knowledge, skills or abilities. I am not my position or role. My essence is deeper. What are the implications for Organization Design, Assessment and Selection?

♦ It is not my nature to be told what to do and to have my choices determined for me. We are equals. Share power. Let me make my own choices and participate in the creation of our collective purpose. What are the implications for Organization Design, Talent and Career Paths and Leadership Competencies?

♦ It is not my nature to be judged and evaluated. I desire acceptance, not approval. Observe and witness for me. Share these reflections with me so I can understand and move to wholeness. What are the implications for Performance Management?

♦ It is not my nature to be "fixed" as part of my development. There is nothing "wrong" with me. I am perfect the way I am. Fully utilize my gifts and strengths: I am hardwired to realize my unique purpose and contribution to life. Accept and help me to become whole. What are the implications for how we approach Learning and Development?

♦ It is not my nature to be compared to others. It is not my nature to become like others. Celebrate my uniqueness. What are the implications for our use of Norms, 360 Assessment, Ratings/Rankings and Rewards Allocation?

Something new is emerging. Hierarchy no longer works effectively. People are saying, *see me for who I am*. Over the last 30 years we have taught the importance of mission, vision, values, collaboration and teamwork. Why? We long to experience oneness. We create diversity and development practices. Why? We desire to honor our uniqueness. What if we used assessment only to honor our unique strengths? We move to participative management. Why? We become open to honor our free will. We look at "symptoms" in our businesses, such as poor morale, and create practices without considering the deep structure of who we really are. We don't fully realize our potential because we don't keep asking, "why?" until we get to the root cause of life, which is love. To find the deepest "why" in choosing any course of action in business, we can ask "How can we support who we *are*?"

We are one with all of creation. We are a unique expression of Source. We have a free will. Through honoring our humanness, we honor our divinity, our oneness, our uniqueness, and our free will. Traditional business approaches and practices have not acknowledged this truth.

AREAS OF TRADITIONAL BUSINESS PRACTICES
WITH POTENTIAL TO ADDRESS OUR DIVINITY

Oneness	Uniqueness	Free Will
Vision	Diversity	Participation
Purpose	Assessment	Communication
Values	Development	Governance
Strategy/Branding	Rewards allocation	Performance
		Management

How can we apply these rules of oneness, uniqueness and free will in leading (and managing) organizations? Our language and actions reveal our beliefs. We lead people and manage work. Managing implies control, which will result in contraction, so I suggest that we remove this language and paradigm from our view of organizations. "Directing" work means to create clarity about our oneness, connection in a common cause, and each individual's contribution. Establishing oneness through Foundational principles enables our uniqueness and free will because we can trust that others will do no harm. Oneness enables employees to exercise uniqueness and free will in the way they do their work.

The power of unlimited growth and expansion that is based in love comes only from freedom of choice, our free will. The business opportunity is to create an environment that brings forth internal commitment and elicits optimal choices from each individual. This creates innovation and new opportunities, opening a world of possibilities. Giving choice creates commitment and the opportunity for expansion and growth.

THE FOCUS OF HUMAN BUSINESS

To support our divinity, the focus of business activities becomes collaboration, connection and community in the creation of products and services that are valued by and provide a benefit to our customers. Motivation is internal and stems from contribution, self-responsibility and growth through purposeful work. Work becomes livelihood, a place for us to develop, to be in service to others and ourselves. Rather than judgment and control, the basic premise of leadership and management practices is acceptance and individual development.

The building blocks of a human-based business are clarity of purpose, networks of relationships/connections and open information sharing. The clarity of business purpose provides a "boundary"; it is the point of "control" for the organization. In their book, *A Simpler Way*, Meg Wheatley and Myron Kellnor-Rogers state that maximum freedom (versus control) comes from deep agreement with and congruence with this purpose. It allows the system to organize itself. The networks and information flow provide opportunity for the generation of new ideas, leading to creativity and innovation in products and services. As we attract and retain more customers with new products and services, financial gain is a by-product.

Leaders help others to discover themselves and contribute based on their own identity/purpose. Power is based on aligning with one's life purpose, one's unique contribution. Uniqueness and diversity are valued as sources of ideas, creativity and innovation.

Measurement is done not for control, but for stewardship so that people can become more self-aware. In addition to results, measures focus on mapping the extent and quality of relationships, since sharing ideas and experience is a source of creativity. Individuals choose their own measures and evaluate their own performance; they do not look to others for approval. Feedback comes from the work itself and through sharing observations without judgment to support self-awareness. Relationships and dialogue are a source of creativity, learning, and mastery of self. Individuals are highly valued as integral to the system, the whole being greater than the sum of the parts.

FOCUS OF HUMAN BUSINESS

Purpose	- Serve and benefit others
Focus of activities	- Collaboration, connection and community - Create valued products and services
Source of "control"	- Internal to the individual and in interaction with system - Self-governance
Source of motivation	- Internal to the individual based in meaning and purpose - Self-determination and development of potential
Leader-employee interaction	- As equals - Self-responsibility and determination - Acceptance and development - Be who you are
Measures of success	- Quality of thinking - Quality of relationships (internal and external) - Quality of actions - Quality of results: self-actualization and self-transcendence, financial performance
Source of power	- Purpose of the organization - Each individual's purpose
Role of profit	- An outcome, not reason for being - One measure of success
View of work	- Whole is greater than the sum of the parts - Place to develop - Place to be in service

Dimensions of Human Business

The Integrated Framework chart (next page) shows us the dimensions to be considered in creating an effective "human" business. This chart is based on Ken Wilbur's "Integral Model of Consciousness" described in his book, *A Theory of Everything*. In our adaptation of Wilbur's model to business, Elizabeth Hall and I included the "Engine of Success" (circle in the center) created by Charles Roe and the Society for Organizational Learning (SoL).

The individual aspects in the top two boxes focus on our uniqueness and free will, essentially the diversity within the organization. The collective aspects in the bottom two boxes serve to create oneness.

Leaders create principles that enable others to act. We can take action to address all four quadrants so that they respect our oneness, uniqueness and free will. The "Engine of Success" in the middle of the chart shows the focus of the adjoining two quadrants: the quality of our thinking, actions, relationships or results. It shows us why we focus on these quadrants and what we can observe to know how we are progressing.

AN INTEGRATED FRAMEWORK: Organization as Collective of Individuals

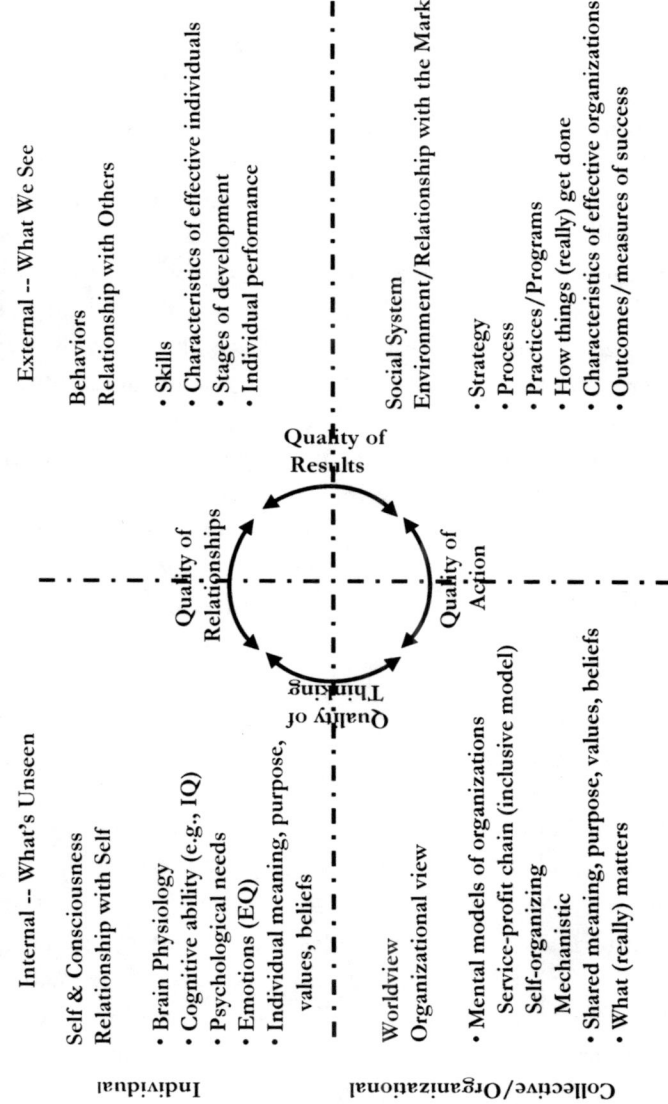

Internal -- What's Unseen

Self & Consciousness
Relationship with Self

- Brain Physiology
- Cognitive ability (e.g., IQ)
- Psychological needs
- Emotions (EQ)
- Individual meaning, purpose, values, beliefs

External -- What We See

Behaviors
Relationship with Others

- Skills
- Characteristics of effective individuals
- Stages of development
- Individual performance

Worldview
Organizational view

- Mental models of organizations
  Service-profit chain (inclusive model)
  Self-organizing
  Mechanistic
- Shared meaning, purpose, values, beliefs
- What (really) matters

Social System
Environment/Relationship with the Market

- Strategy
- Process
- Practices/Programs
- How things (really) get done
- Characteristics of effective organizations
- Outcomes/measures of success

Individual

Collective/Organizational

Quality of Results

Quality of Relationships

Quality of Action

Quality of Thinking

Applying the Truths to Organizations: Oneness, Uniqueness and Free Will

Returning to the model, the Energy of Business Success, in the preceding chapter (see page 53), we see that our Foundational principles create our oneness, our shared meaning of why we exist as an organization and what we are choosing to manifest or create together. Vision is the desired end-state that encompasses our Purpose, Values and Strategy/Branding. Purpose is the unique value we create that is in service to others. It provides the clarity of our identity – who we are and why we are here – for both individuals and organizations. Values are our shared beliefs about what is important. Strategy is our unique positioning in the marketplace that differentiates us from other organizations (e.g., quality, product, cost). Branding is what we stand for, our promise to our customers. Organization Design (structure and work design) provides purpose and interdependence describing overall contributions to our oneness. It is based in equality and shared power with active participation in establishing both direction and decisions, which foster collaboration and self-governance.

Our Operational Practices based in the Foundational principles connect individuals with our oneness and support uniqueness and free will. The catalyst is communication that includes broad and open dialogue and that honors our uniqueness and free will and builds collective wisdom. Through communication we facilitate freedom and discretion in determining actions. Performance and Contribution Enhancement begins with placement that enables us to use our gifts and fulfill our individual purpose. Our passions, capabilities and skills allow us to manifest our unique purpose. Our career paths provide individual choices that respect and support our purpose, connection and development.

Engagement and Development are achieved through observational, non-judgmental coaching that elicits our inner knowledge to achieve optimal performance. We foster individual self-awareness and transformation, becoming fully conscious of self as divine. Our measures enable us to self-monitor. We maximize each other's contribution based on our capability, knowledge and strengths. We encourage learning and mastery through personal experience and reflection, building on what is already known. There is an annual renewal process that reaffirms the core purpose of each group and position so that we tap into our boundless human energy. Shared rewards affirm each individual and his or her contribution to our oneness.

THE FUTURE

We no longer simply consider our positioning in the marketplace to sell *to* customers. Sales becomes about "attracting" customers who desire our products or services. We look to create connection with their essence, honoring their uniqueness and free will. The sales process enables our customers to experience our oneness with them and to experience the essence of our products and services, our brand(s) identity(ies).

We no longer simply consider marketing as "spinning" our aspirations. Marketing becomes an integrated communication path between the leaders of the business and its customers.

We no longer simply consider finance as an accounting process or budget monitoring that confine or limit our possibilities and choices. Finance becomes a means to ensure the flow of abundance. This flow is an exchange process of value between the business and the marketplace and among the functional areas inside of the organization. The purpose of the finance process becomes to expand potential and increase creative possibilities.

We no longer simply consider people as resources to be managed and "boxed" into organizational charts. Rather, people become stewards of our brand. Their talents create the product or service that customers experience as the manifestation of the brand(s) promises(s). "Human Resources" becomes "Human Wholeness," supporting leaders and creating practices so that employees feel valued for their uniqueness and grow and experience fully who they are. The customer experience that results from engaged talent draws new customers to us and enables us to retain the customers we have.

Organizational change is integral to how we lead and manage, accepting that the nature of the human experience *is* change. Leadership in Service to Life in and of itself fosters both individual and organizational change and we enable transformation when we establish:

♦ Clarity of our oneness: Vision, Purpose, Values, Strategy/Branding, Organizational Design and Governance.

♦ Consistency that enables our uniqueness: Disciplined, conscious attention and action within and across individuals and over time. Consistent actions include communication and operating practices. Shared understanding comes through dialogue and participation.

♦ Commitment through free choice: Engaged emotions, the desire and motivation that come though active participation and co-creation.

The chart on the following page summarizes the application of the universal principles to Leadership in Service to Life business practices. Let us create businesses where we join together as one, celebrate each individual's unique contribution, and give each individual true choice in their experiences with us.

The good news is we have solid places to look for guidance in our practices. Positive Organizational Scholarship, an emerging area of research based at the University of Michigan Business School, and established methods, such as Appreciative Inquiry, with research based at Case Western University, show us the effectiveness of affirming life within business. While they don't use my language, they do give us practices that are generative and life supporting. Practices that are based in:

Oneness. Uniqueness. Free will. Three simple truths.

APPLICATION OF UNIVERSAL SPIRITUAL PRINCIPLES TO BUSINESS LEADERSHIP

Divine Nature	Psychological Needs That Guide Union with Source	Areas of Organizational Practice	Leadership in Service to Life Practices
Oneness	Connection & Participation – To be part of something larger than ourselves	Strategy/Branding Values Organization Design Governance Communication	Equality & shared power Active participation Broad & open dialogue
Uniqueness	Purpose & Meaning – To bring value & benefit to others; to enhance life	Purpose/Mission	Universal clarity of organizational identity Clarity of individual purpose & Contribution
Free Will	Self-determination & Choice – To choose our life experiences	Performance Contribution & Enhancement Planning & Monitoring	Choose own career progression Feedback from work & self-awareness Stewardship focused
Return to Source	Growth & Creativity – To expand who we know ourselves to be	Engagement & Development	Expand strengths Personal experience with reflection Non-judgmental coaching Build collective wisdom
Unconditional, Selfless Love	Respect, Acceptance & Appreciation – To be appreciated for our uniqueness and be loved	Leadership Participation Shared Rewards	Roles enable use of strengths to fulfill purpose Affirm contribution and purpose

... Work is love made visible.

Kahlil Gibran

In that moment when our desire to do and be the best we can grows stronger than our fear of failure – in that solitary moment – greatness rises up within us to take command and we may dare to do the impossible. It is in that moment that possibility is born.

Kate Nowak

CHAPTER REFLECTIONS

What was your "ah-ha" moment? What did you read that validates or changes how you think about organizational practices?

What are you going to do differently or what actions are you going to take as a result of these insights?

7

EPILOGUE: UTOPIA IN 2013

The world we have made as a result of the level of thinking we have done thus far creates problems we cannot solve at the same level of thinking at which we created them.

Albert Einstein

The Law of Attraction says that like attracts like. Love attracts love. Fear attracts fear. The Rule of Relationship and Reciprocity says that what we give, we will receive. Respect brings respect. Trust brings trust. Inner peace brings peace to the world.

We have the power, one person at a time, to change the human experience to one of universal peace and prosperity. It comes from how each of us chooses to relate to others and to all of creation.

We have a free will and can choose either love or fear. The choice is ours. Spirit does not care, because it is all part of Spirit's experience through each of us.

Cosmic Consciousness or Enlightenment is our complete union with our divine self. It is the total awareness of Source within and acting only from this state of love.

According to predictions of many ancient calendars, the world as we know it will cease to exist in 2012. This does not necessarily mean that we will destroy the world, only that the world we create by our choices and actions will be different from the world we know today.

Patricia Aburdene (*Megatrends 2010: The Rise of Conscious Capitalism*) and Judi Neal (*Edgewalkers: People and Organizations That Take Risks, Build Bridges and Break New Ground*) both describe business leaders who come from a spiritual center. Many others are actively working to address our humanness and connection with creation. Both science (e.g., quantum physics) and psychology (e.g., positive psychology) are expanding our understanding and showing us the way.

Utopia in 2013 is not outside of our grasp. When we look at recent history and the fall of apartheid in South Africa, the tearing down of the Berlin Wall and reunification of Germany, and the dissolution of the Soviet Union, these three world-changing events came without prediction and had instantaneous impact. We can change the world one person at a time, starting with ourselves. Business is an ideal place to begin because in business we naturally come together to create something of value for others.

Utopia is both a possible and a probable future. We *are* all leaders. The world will become what we *choose* to make it. Thank you for allowing me to share my insights for life and business. So, with the dawn of 2007, you can ask yourself:

Am I willing to reconnect to my divinity so I may lead others to theirs?

Am I co-creating with the energy of love?

Am I willing to be a leader and meet the challenges of business and global transformation?

Am I willing to be a leader in service to life?

Spirit, thank you for our healing and our path home. Through the power of our choice of divine love, we all know self-forgiveness, and our hearts open to unconditional love.

Lucira

By the will of Abba – Mother – Father – Creator – God; through the unconditional love of the Christ within; through wisdom and truth of Spirit within; we create heaven on earth. It is so.

Lucira

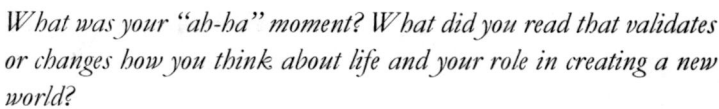

CHAPTER REFLECTIONS

What was your "ah-ha" moment? What did you read that validates or changes how you think about life and your role in creating a new world?

What are you going to do differently or what actions are you going to take as a result of these insights?

RESOURCES

These organizations and sources were mentioned in the book, so to facilitate your desire to learn more, they are listed below.

Appreciative Inquiry
appreciativeinquiry.case.edu

Association for Spirit at Work
www.SpiritatWork.org

Brain Physiology
For a simple, clear and brief explanation of the evolution and physiology of the human brain, see Chapter 2 in Daniel Goleman's book, *Emotional Intelligence*

Heartmath
www.Heartmath.com

Positive Organizational Scholarship
www.bus.umich.edu/Positive/WhatisPOS/

Society for Organizational Learning (SoL)
www.solonline.org

Spiral Dynamics
www.wie.org/spiral/

ABOUT THE AUTHOR

Jane C. Nebelung has nearly 30 years of experience in partnering with executives and managers to improve their business results and to implement change successfully. Her experience includes working with companies such as Liz Claiborne, CIGNA, Aetna, Texas Instruments, the Bureau of Business Practices, and LIMRA International.

Jane has worked as an executive-level partner in the fields of Organization Development/Effectiveness and Change Implementation. In these roles, she is noted as a business leader, architect, facilitator and coach for key strategic initiatives in Fortune 100 companies that resulted in employee engagement and optimal performance, customer retention and sustained business growth and profitability. Jane is also recognized for exceptional contributions, including top-line growth and bottom-line impact, vision and innovation, strategic and tactical leadership, collaboration, and mentoring colleagues and staff.

In her most recent corporate role, she headed Strategic Learning and Change for CIGNA Retirement & Investment Services. At Aetna for nine years, she held various positions, including Head of Learning and Performance for Aetna Customer Service and Director of Organization Capability. With LIMRA, Jane worked with companies on their marketing management practices to increase sales.

Jane engages in life and her work from a spiritual foundation and perspective. She is the founder and president of Nebelung Associates, LLC, working with executives to expand business value and growth by aligning organizational actions with leader intentions through Thought Partnership and by building Leadership Mastery founded in Universal Spiritual Principles.

Nebelung is a graduate of Emmanuel College in Boston with a B.S. in Psychology. She has her M.A. in Psychology from the University of Hartford and is certified in Executive Coaching by the Professional School of Psychology in Sacramento, California.

Jane is the author of more than 50 business and professional articles and presentations. She is a frequently invited guest instructor in the executive business programs at Central Connecticut State University and the University of New Haven, and serves as an adjunct faculty member at Quinnipiac University. She is a member of the American Psychological Association (APA), the Society for Industrial Organizational Psychology (SIOP), the World Future Society, the Institute of Noetic Sciences (IONS), and the Association for Spirit at Work.

Jane lives in Niantic, Connecticut with her husband of 17 years, Alexander.

Lucira, quoted in this book, is Jane's divine self, her connection to Spirit. The name means the Bringer of the Power of Light. These passages were received in meditation.

Jane welcomes your comments and can be reached at:

Jane.Nebelung@snet.net
www.LeadershipinServicetoLife.com

Printed in the United States
77275LV00001B/397-495